T0109180

GET OUT!
I'm Trying to F**k Your Mother

Copyright © 2012 Tribeca Publishing
Illustrations copyright © 2012 Michel Roseau
All rights reserved.

Manufactured in Mexico
February 2012

ISBN 978-1-935703-59-4

10 9 8 7 6 5 4 3 2 1

www.getoutthebook.com

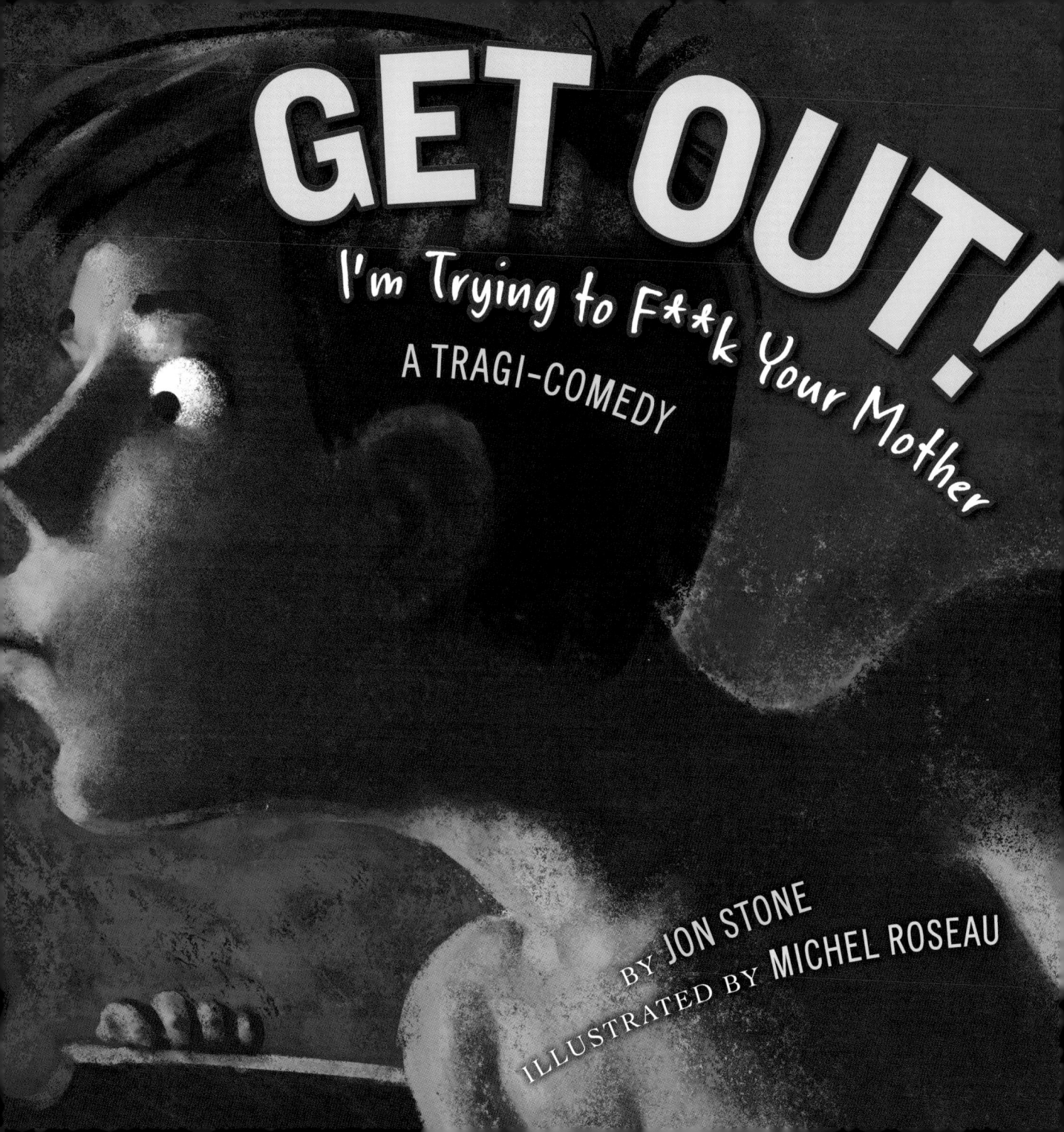
GET OUT!
I'm Trying to F**k Your Mother
A TRAGI-COMEDY
BY JON STONE
ILLUSTRATED BY MICHEL ROSEAU

The kids are all sleeping.
Let's go to bed early.
What peeks through the door?
A head that is curly.

March back to your bed—
let's end this charade.
You're cute as a button,
but Dad's getting laid.

Now what? Little footsteps —
and a whisper so sweet,
as small, pudgy fingers
tug at the sheet.

I'll stay under here
until we both smother.
I'm not coming out
'til I fuck your mother.

I'm not hurting Mommy,
it's a fun grown-up game.
Give me a second—
I'll come up with a name...

We played the same game
to make you—in this bed!
Right now I'm wishing
I had a blow job instead.

I'm THIRSTY!

Sorry Mom woke you,
she's a bit of a moaner.
I'd run to the kitchen,
but you'd see Daddy's boner.

There's nothing to fear.
Close your eyes and rest.
(Though you might see a ghost
before I see Mommy's breasts.)

That growl is my stomach—
not a monster that roars.
And the sound in the driveway?
Daddy's off to find whores.

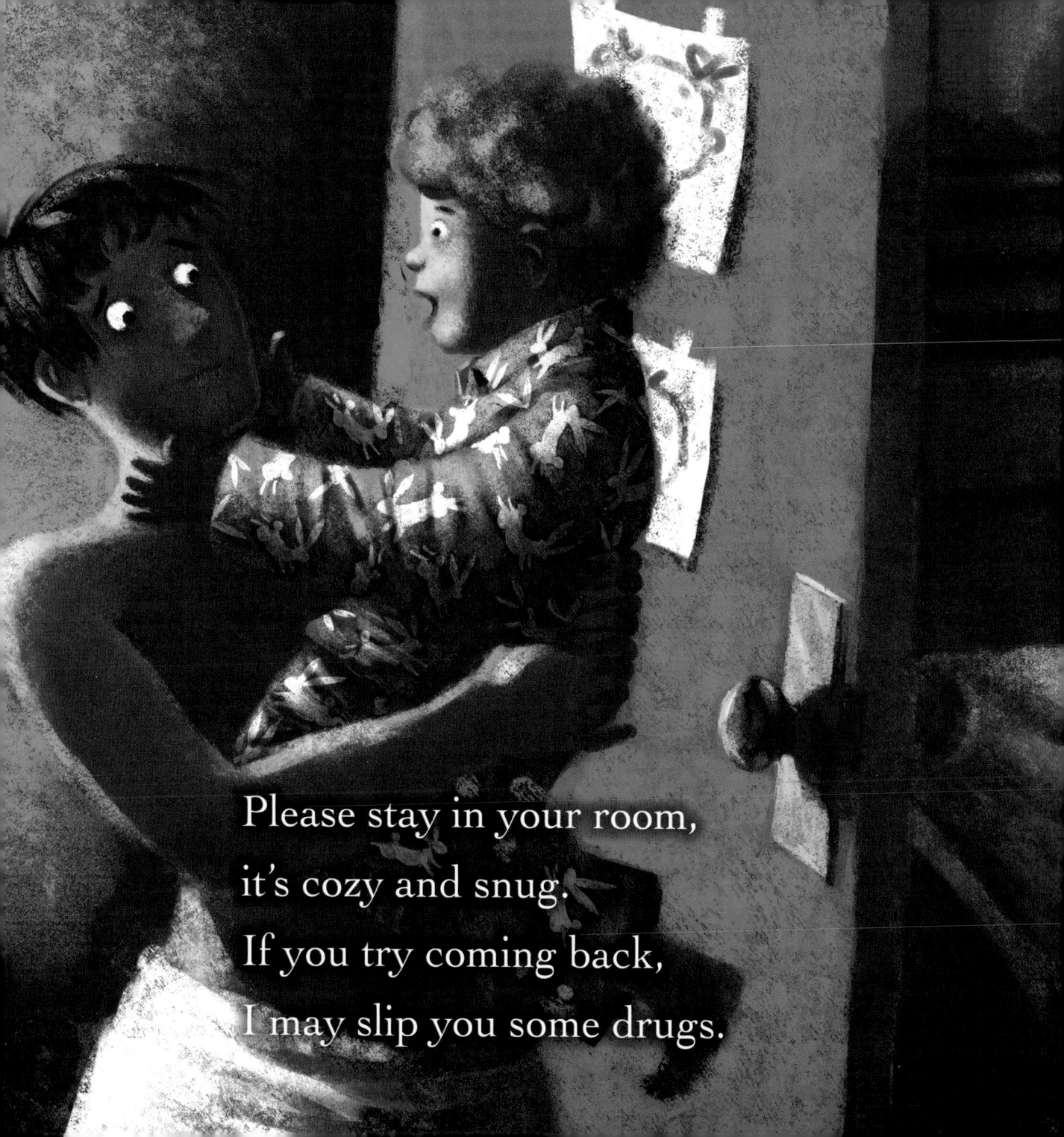

Please stay in your room,
it's cozy and snug.
If you try coming back,
I may slip you some drugs.

Of course Daddy loves you,
and I'm thrilled you were born.
It's just that I miss
getting off without porn.

I've read so many books:
Seuss, Steig, *Goodnight Moon*.
But now you need sleep,
and Daddy needs poon.

Harold and his crayon
that makes things real?
I've got something purple
for Mommy to feel.

The Little Engine that Could?
I totally relate.
I *know* that I can
with just 10 minutes straight.

Now the big one wants in
on the family bed!
You'll all be in college
before Daddy gets head.
Stomach...
pain... dying...

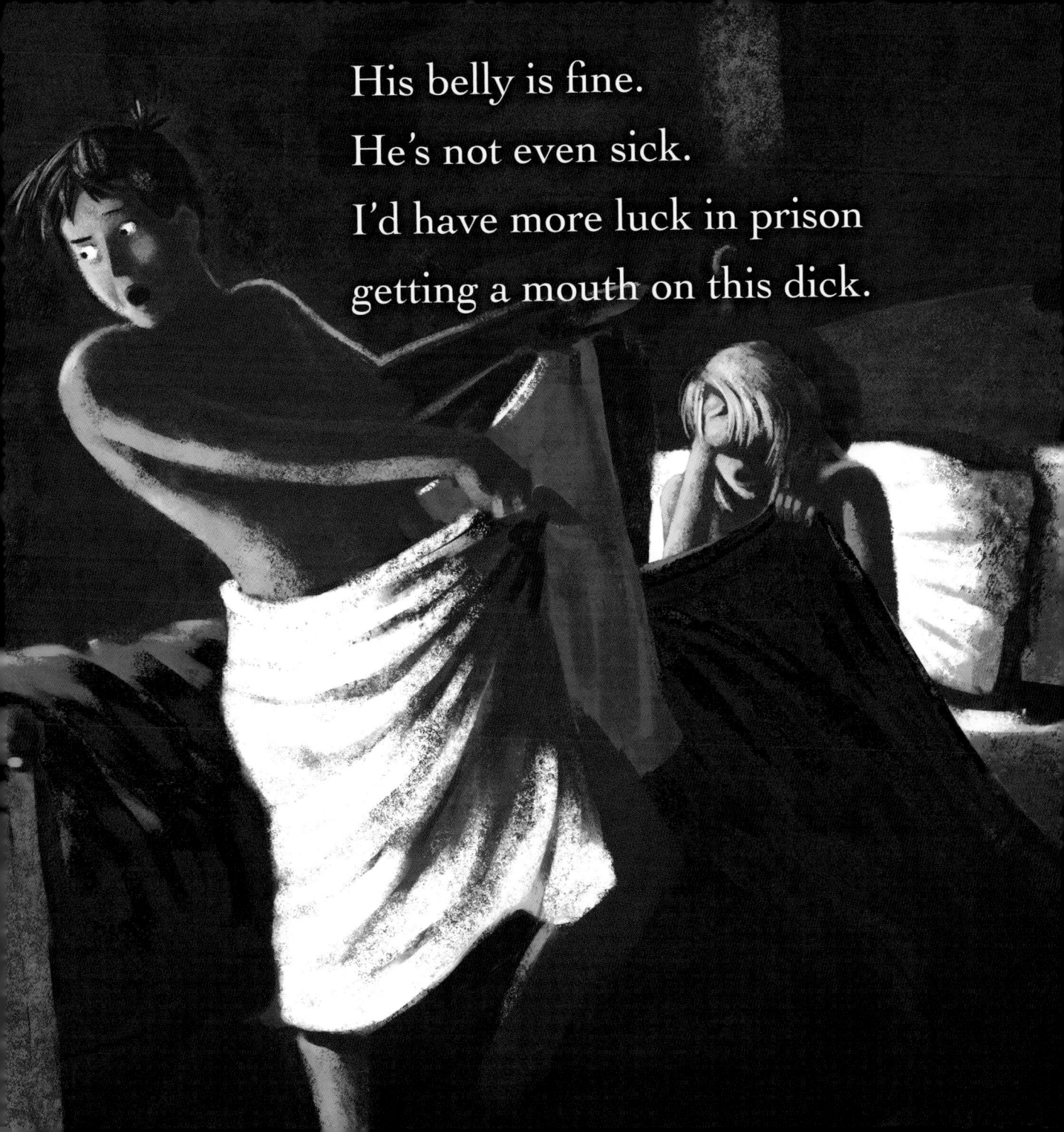

His belly is fine.
He's not even sick.
I'd have more luck in prison
getting a mouth on this dick.

Have candy. Some ice cream?
TV. Bubble gum!
Just give us five minutes,
so Daddy can come.

That was SO NOT five minutes
'til you pounded and screamed.
You may be in our bed,
but Mom's still getting reamed.

You can't all have to go
at the very same time.
Is this some kind of
Kafka-esque nursery rhyme?

You took over our bed,
now we're stuck on the tile
You had drinks, you had treats.
I'll have mine doggy style.

Babe, Daddy loves you…
And your sister. And brother!
But GO AWAY PLEASE.
I'm trying to fuck your mother.

Mom? Dad...?
I hear a scary noise!

Father? The door seems to be stuck...

We're finally alone!
I'm so happy I could weep…

Get the fuck off of me—
I'm trying to sleep!

Lotion